ROMANIA
The most beautiful places

Descrierea CIP a Bibliotecii Naţionale a României
OVIDIU MORAR
România / Ovidiu Morar; traducere în limba engleză: Alina Cârâc,
graf.: Adrian Sorin Georgescu; foto: Ovidiu Morar, Dan Ioan Dinescu,
Mircea Savu, Ştefan Petrescu; - Bucureşti: ed.: NOI Media Print, 2007

ISBN 973-7959-56-6

I.   Alina Cârâc (trad.)
II.   Georgescu, Adrian Sorin (graf)
III.   Morar, Ovidiu (foto)
IV.   Dinescu, Dan Ioan (foto)
V.   Savu, Mircea (foto)
VI.   Ştefan Petrescu (foto)
VII.   Daniel Focşa / Dana Voiculescu (text)

Contents

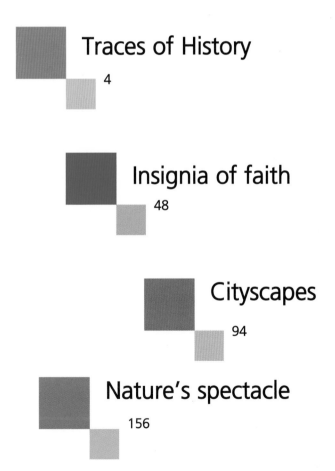

Traces of History

Histria Vestiges

Histria, baptized after the Greek name of the Danube (Istros), was founded on the western shore of the Black Sea in the mid 7th century B.C. (specifically, in the year 657 B. C., according to historian Eusebius) by Greek colonists coming from Miletus. It is the oldest Greek colony in the west of Pontus Euxinus, and at the same time the oldest documented town on the territory of Romania. Last but not least, Histria is one of the biggest archaeological sites in this country. The citadel prospered for a millennium, starting with the Greek period down to the Roman-Byzantine times. Histria's economic development began to dwindle the moment sand gradually closed the gulf where the colony was located. Inroads turned it to ruin, round 242, and subsequently the citadel was completely abandoned in the 7th century.

The archaeological digs began in 1914 under the supervision of the great Romanian historian and archaeologist Vasile Parvan, and they provided extremely rich archaeological material, part of it now on display in the museum arranged close to the citadel.

Ruins of the Roman baths

Daco-Roman Vestiges at Sarmizegetusa

Two thousand years ago, on a plateau in Orastie Mountains there rose a complex of Dacian fortifications (Sarmizegetusa, Blidaru, Piatra Rosie, Costesti, Capalna), with Sarmizegetusa Regia the most important military, religious and political center of Dacia. Around A.D. 107, after the Dacians' defeat by the Romans, the capital of the new Roman province moved 40 kilometers away from the ruins of Sarmizegetusa Regia, and acquired the name of Colony Ulpia Trajana Augusta Dacica Sarmizegetusa. The city developed until A. D. 271 when the Roman authorities withdrew from Dacia. Vestiges of the amphitheater, the forum, and the baths, of public and private edifices have been preserved to this day, all of huge archaeological and historical interest.

The Roman forum, fragment c pilaster capital and sculpted cornice

Ulpia Trajana Sarmizegetusa: the circular amphitheater

The Cistercian Abbey of Carta

The Evangelical Church of Carta belongs to a former Cistercian (a Catholic order of monks, originating in France) abbey. The monastery was founded in 1202, and remade between 1242 and 1250, following the destruction wrecked by the big Tartar invasion. In 1474, the King of Hungary, Matei Corvin dismantled the monastery, and put the building in the administration of the Catholic Church of Sibiu. Subsequently, it became an Evangelical parish. It is a representative monument of early Transylvanian Gothic, bearing influence on medieval architecture in the entire southeastern part of the province.

Throughout its existence, the Cistercian abbey of Carta held a major role in the political, economic, and cultural history of medieval Transylvania.

The Cistercian Abbey of Carta. Only the choir, where the present Evangelical Church serves, has been preserved from the old edifice

The Peasant Citadel of Rasnov

Erected in the 14th century, the citadel was expanded, consolidated and remade until the 18th century. Situated on a 150-m high rock, close to the commercial route connecting Transylvania to Wallachia, the city withheld numerous sieges, serving as protection and shelter for the inhabitants of the area. To this end, small houses were put up within the citadel meant to shelter the population and their assets, as well as a school, a chapel, and a cattle fold. The lack of water limited the period of refuge in the citadel in case of a siege. That is why in 1625 a well began to be dug in rock, inside the city. Today, Rasnov is one of the best preserved citadels in Transylvania. In recent years a private entrepreneur took it over and turned it into a very attractive tourist target.

Righ
Overall view

Le
Exterior wal

p. 14-1
Interior detail

The Slimnic Citadel

On the road from Sibiu to Medias, the ruins of the citadel on the Slimnic hilltop tower over the locality with the same name, a picturesque addition to the natural scenery.

The construction began in the 14th century and was expanded until the 16th century. Initially, the fortification sheltered a Gothic chapel in the northern area, later turned into a defense tower. A three-nave edifice (a Gothic church is composed of a nave, choir and apse) separates the city in two distinct precincts. With the construction of the basilica, the interior fortification was also repaired and expanded, being endowed with crenels and defense towers in order to withhold attacks. Which it did, several times. In 1706, during the Kurutzi war, the citadel was set on fire and abandoned.

Ruins of the citadel

The Fortified Church of Prejmer

The Clock Tower of the church

The Evangelical church of Prejmer (Tartlau in German), in Gothic style with Cistercian influences, was erected in the 13th century. Only two fresco parts have been preserved of the initial painting that covered the entire church. The triptych Gothic altar, painted on both sides, goes back to 1450.

A fortified wall, 12-m tall and 3-4 meters thick, surrounds the edifice, which houses 272 rooms disposed in honeycomb, on four levels. The rooms served as storage place for vittles in times of peace, and as dwellings in time of siege.

Within the citadel there is a Saxon ethnographic museum that displays cult items, clothing, painted furniture, and ceramics.

Overall view

Honeycomb dwellings on the precinct wall. During a siege, they served as shelter for the entire community, and in periods of peace they were used as storage rooms.

Interior view. Vault with terracotta ribbings and organ on the background

Interior view.
Gothic decorations

The Hunedoara Citadel

The castle was erected in the 14th century on the spot of a stone fortification. In 1409, King Sigismund of Hungary bestowed the citadel on a nobleman, Voicu. His son, Iancu of Hunedoara brought radical changes to the citadel turning it into a castle that was equally a strategic stronghold and a lavish habitation. Matei Corvin, the son of Iancu of Hunedoara, rebuilt the northern wing of the castle, while in the 17th century Prince Gabriel Bethlen contributed several modifications inspired from late Renaissance.

The edifice, also known as the Hunyadi or Corvin castle is an imposing construction, with tall, variously colored roofs, with towers, small and big, and lacy windows and balconies. The castle features a combination of Renaissance, Gothic, and Baroque architectural elements.

At present, exhibitions and shows of pre-classical and old music are held in the halls of the castle.

Partial view: the acces
bridge, resting on fou
massive stone pillars
mention should be made
of the Gate Tower and
the Mace Towe

Fragment from the neo-Gothic gallery

Neamt Citadel

The citadel of Neamt was erected during the reign of Petru I Musat, being one of the best fortified Moldavian medieval cities. The emplacement of the citadel assured it excellent defense possibilities. The city plan looks like a quadrilateral with uneven sides, the construction being adapted to the soil. The defense towers were directly included into the walls and not corbelled out like with other citadels. During the reign of Stephen the Great the walls were further elevated, a new, deeper defense ditch was dug, flanked by four bastions provided with crenels and slim windows. Access to the citadel was made on an arched bridge, supported by 11 stone pillars, and with the last part mobile. After 1717, the citadel lost its defensive importance, and consequently, in 1718 the Turks ordered it to be demolished.

Bird's eye view

Interior detail

The Suceava Citadel

Interior details

The citadel was built in the late 14th century, during the reign of Petru I Musat who moved the Princely residence from Siret to Suceva, for two centuries (1388-1566). The citadel flourished considerably during the epoch of Stephen the Great, who expanded its precincts, strengthened it by adding tall, thick walls, and semi-circular bastions, and also widened the defense ditches. Then he restored the inside halls (sleeping chambers, chapel, ammunition and foodstuffs storages) for the soldiers and his family.

In 1675, the Ottoman Porte ordered the destruction of the citadel. A few years later a powerful earthquake led to the collapse of the entire northern wing. Today, the city of Suceava, partly restored, represents an extensive open-air museum, a formidable tourist attraction for those interested in Moldavia's medieval history.

Overall view of Moldavia's seat city

27

Bran Castle

The citadel of Bran, erected around 1212, in wood, (probably by the Teutonic Knights) and replaced by the Saxons with a stone structure, in 1377, served military as well as customs purposes. Between 1498 and 1877, the city belonged to Brasov, fulfilling commercial and administrative roles. In token of gratitude for the contribution to the achievement of the Great Union of 1918, Brasov's town council donated the citadel to Queen Maria of Romania, on December 1, 1920. Between 1920 and 1927, the royal family used Bran as summer residence that boasted promenade alleys, a lake, fountains, and terraces. In 1938, Queen Maria bequeathed Bran castle and the respective domain to her daughter, Princess Ileana. In 1948, the communist regime sent the royal family into exile and confiscated the castle. In 1956, it was opened as a Museum of Medieval History and Art, housing collections of period furniture and old weapons.

Right
Overall view

Left
Exterior details

p. 30-3
Interior detail

The Princely Court of Targoviste

The Princely Court of Targoviste is the best preserved medieval ensemble in Romania. Achieved in stages, between 1396 and 1698, it was Princely residence and seat for thirty-three rulers of Wallachia. The ensemble includes the Princely palace, erected between the 15th and the 17th centuries (ruined today); the big Princely church (1584), with interior painting dating to 1697 (achieved during the reign of Prince Constantin Brancoveanu, it features the amplest gallery of portraits of Romanian sovereign); the small Princely church or the St Friday church, built in the 15th century, and preserved without alterations to this day; the Chindia Tower, from 1460, erected by Vlad Tepes (The Impaler); and the Balasa House (1656) set up as an asylum for the poor and a guest house.

The Princely palace consists of two wings, one from the time of Mircea the Old, and the second larger one from the reign of Petru Cercel, who moved the capital of Wallachia to Targoviste, in 1584.

Chindia Tower (27 m), situate on the northwestern side o the Princely Cour

The Princely Court: ruins of the palace and the big princely churcl

The Maldaresti Cula (Mansion)

Cula is a word of Turkish inspiration (kule means defense tower) designating a boyar's fortified house, with one or two floors, and an observation belfry on the last level. Such types of small citadel were erected in the early 18th century in the region of Oltenia, and in northwestern Muntenia with a view to offering protection against Turkish gangs. Cula Greceanu, alongside the Cula Duca, belongs to the Maldaresti museum complex, and is one of the oldest constructions of the kind in the country. Characteristic for an Oltenian cula is the porch on the higher floor. Its elegant trilobate arcades rest on short and thick cylindrical columns, and evince influences of Brancovan architecture. The wall of the stair well features shooting holes. The cellar represents an important area of the cula, its major characteristic being the central pillar supporting the vaulted ceiling.

In time, the defensive role of the cula diminished, and it remained just a token of its owner's belonging to a high social class.

The Fagaras Citadel

The Fagaras Citadel was constructed on a swampy plot of land, in 1310, on orders from Prince Ladislau Apor, first in wood, then in stone, in 1538. In the 15th century the citadel had the geometric form of an irregular quadrilateral, defended by a barbequenne tower. In the 16th century, the citadel was turned into a Princely castle with a strong exterior fortification.

The 17th century marked an acme in the citadel's evolution to the shape it takes today. Bastions were erected, floors were added, the ditch surrounding the fortification was filled with water (following its connection, through a secret channel, to the river Olt), and stylistic transformations were performed (the castle was brought on a par with Renaissance aesthetics).

In the 18th century, the Austrians took over the citadel and turned it into a garrison. In 1965, the citadel of Fagaras became a museum.

Overall view

Interior yard and one of the bastions

Brancoveanu Palace, the
western arcade

The Mogosoaia Palace lies in a splendid park, a few kilometers away from Bucharest, on the banks of the Mogosoaia Lake. Prince Constantin Brancoveanu erected the building in 1702 for his son, Stefan, on the pattern of the Potlogi palace. Considered an architectural gem, the palace combines Wallachian decorative elements, with Byzantine and Italian Renaissance ones. It presents a regular rectangular plan on three levels: the cellar (vaulted, with semispherical calottes), the ground floor, and the first floor. Access to the dwelling floor is made through the grand yard, via a belfry situated in the middle of the main façade, supported by eight stone columns, and featuring a richly ornamented banister. Both the balcony and the upper rooms were initially decorated with Oriental stucco and murals representing the members of the Princely family as well as historical scenes. The most refined architectural element of the

The princely kitchen

palace is the Venetian-inspired loggia, with trilobate arcades supported by columns, and situated on the lake façade. Within the interior yard can be seen the kitchen and the icehouse.

In 1912, the palace became the property of Princess Martha Bibescu, who restored it, bringing masters from Italy, who gave the building a marked Venetian air, coating the façades with exposed bricks. In 1945, Martha Bibescu managed to include the palace on the list of historical monuments. As a result, the communist regime did not confiscate it. In 1993, the Ministry of Culture initialed a foundation here, the National Cultural Center of Mogosoaia, where commedia dell'arte shows and concerts are held.

Guest wing and loggia
Architecture detail

Guest wing or Vila Elchingen
(the 19th century), general view

The Peles Complex

General view

In 1873, in a savage and picturesque area, close to Sinaia Monastery works began on the summer residence of Prince Carol I of Romania, on a plot privately owned by the sovereign. Ten years later the castle was inaugurated officially, but works to extend and improve the royal castle continued to 1914. Next to Peles, the smaller castles of Pelisor and Foisor were erected, as well as the guard corps, the administration, the royal stables, and the electric station. Created by architects Wilhelm Doderer, Johannes Schultz, Karel Liman, and prestigious decorators like J. D. Heymann of Hamburg, A. Bembe of Mains, and Bernhard Ludwig of Vienna, the castle played an important political and cultural role, along the years the royal family having here as guests numerous Romanian artists.

The castle has been open since the time of King Carol I, for visits of the hall of weapons, the council hall, the old music hall, the Moorish hall, the Turkish salon, the theater hall, the dining rooms, and the Florentine hall.

Statue of King Carol I (1866-1914)

43

Statues in the Guard Corps and the Clock Tower of the castle

Alba Iulia – The Union City

As a result of Romania's participation in the First World War, the provinces in the Austro-Hungarian and Russian Empires, inhabited mostly by Romanians, were joined to the country. King Ferdinand I and Queen Maria were crowned in Alba Iulia, on October 15, 1922, as sovereigns of Greater Romania. Alba Iulia was chosen city of the Union because of its symbolical character, given that here Prince Michael the Brave achieved the first union of the Romanian Principalities in 1601.

The Eastern Orthodox Coronation Cathedral, also called the Reintegration Cathedral, dedicated to the Holy Trinity, was built between 1921 and 1922, in the style of the old churches of Wallachia. It stands close to the old Roman Catholic Cathedral. Smaller turrets and a 58-m tall belfry flank its central tower. Architect Victor G. Ieremia made the designs. The painting is the creation of the celebrated artist Costin Petrescu.

Together with the Union Hall, the cathedral is a true symbol of the Great Union.

Coronation Cathedral

The Union Museum, the Union Hall

Insignia of Faith

The Densus Church

Dedicated to Saint Nicholas, the church situated in the vicinity of vestiges from the Roman Dacia capital is one of the oldest Eastern Orthodox abodes in Romania. It was erected in the 13th century in stone and marble, with columns coming from the ruins of Ulpia Trajana Sarmizegetusa. The Roman stone was used both as a resistance and decorative element. Murals inside the church adorn the altar apse, the eastern walls of the naos, and parts of the central pillars. The church was painted around 1443 by Stephen the Painter, his signature being still visible under the southeastern window of the apse.

With a unique architectural style, the church looks a little quaint, its atypical shape arising controversies among historians. Some opine that it is a former pagan temple, aggrandized and altered to fit the Christian cult, while others believe it is a Roman mausoleum turned into a church.

St. Nicholas Church
view from the ea

Le
Interior of the nave. Slab wit
Roman inscriptio

Righ
Interior yar

The Cozia Monastery

Church of Cozia Monastery,
view from the southeast

Cozia Monastery is one of the oldest Romanian monastic settlements in the land, a foundation of Prince Mircea the Old, dated to 1387-1388. Once it bore the name of Nucet. Sitting on the banks of the Olt, a little higher up than the river gorges, Cozia was repaired, enlarged, and beautified by Prince Neagoe Basarab (1517), and royal sommelier Serban Cantacuzino (1706-1707). The cell wings surround the major precinct on three sides.

The big church, in Byzantine style, is erected in stone alternating with brick, and on the outside decorated with stone sculptures. The porch, in Brancovan style, was added in 1707. The abode shelters the remains of Prince Mircea the Old and of abbess Teofana, mother of Prince Michael the Brave.

Between 1542 and 1543, Radu Paisie erected the infirmary church, outstanding by its architecture. The original 16th century painting has been excellently preserved inside.

Cozia Monastery, overall view

Inner yard and the infirmary church

Putna Monastery

Among the most important foundations of Prince Stephen the Great, Putna Monastery shelters the sovereign's tomb as the abode was devised from the start as a Princely necropolis. Situated 72 kilometers from the Seat of Suceava, the church of Putna monastery was erected between 1466 and 1469. Next came the Princely House (1473), the cells, the defense walls with the respective towers, and the Treasury Tower; the works ended in 1481. The church is dedicated to the Dormition of the Virgin, and was remade by Princes Vasile Lupu and Istrate Dabija, between 1654 and 1662. The only construction from the time of Stephen to have been fully preserved is the Treasury Tower.

Besides including the tombs of Stephen the Great and Petru Rares, the monastery church is also the last resting place of many other Princes and Princesses of the Musatin dynasty.

Bird's eye view from the northeast

57

Window frame. Details

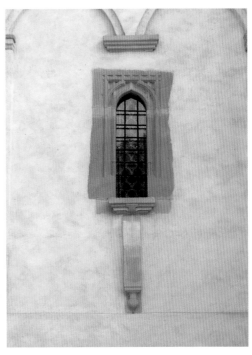

The Patrauti Church

The smallest of the foundations laid by Stephen the Great, the church of Patrauti was erected in 1487. Dedicated to the Elevation of the Holy Cross, the church is at the same time the oldest building ordered by the Voivode that has preserved its initial shape, and the only one meant to be a monastery of nuns. The church architecture combines Gothic, Byzantine, and Renaissance elements. The interior painting was achieved right after the church was terminated. Mention should be made of the votive picture in the naos representing the Prince and his family, and the ample fresco in the pronaos entitled the Cavalcade of the Military Saints. The exterior painting was made after 1550. Fragments from the fresco with the Last Judgment have also been preserved.

The church belfry was put up in the 18ᵗʰ century and it bears strong Maramures influences.

Patrauti Church (148
view from the southwe

Cavalcade of the Holy Cros
Detail of interior mural

Voronet Monastery

The monastery church
seen from the southeast

Prince Stephen the Great erected the abode in 1488. Dedicated to Saint George, the church is famous for its outer and inner painting, achieved later, between 1534-1535, in the time of Petru Rares. The monumental frescoes have a light blue background, the celebrated Voronet blue. The fresco on the western façade of the church (1534-1535) depicts the Last Judgment. The composition takes the whole western wall of the porch. The solution used to create the porch was original, the architecture being visibly subordinated to the painted decoration: the western wall is compact, pierced by no opening. In 1547, metropolitan Grigorie Rosca added a closed porch to the church, with exterior painting by master Marcu. The pronaos was painted in 1550. Dismantled as monastery in 1986, the abode was reopened in 1989, and is today on the UNESCO world heritage list.

The Tree of Jesse, fresco on the
southern wall

Moldovita Monastery

Next to the ruins of the monastery founded between 1402-1410 by Prince Alexander the Kind, Petru Rares erected, in 1532, the present monastery, made up of a church dedicated to the Annunciation, of cells, and a Princely house. Strong walls with defense towers surround the entire ensemble.

In point of architecture, the church has the traditional trefroiled plan with five rooms separated by compact walls, pierced by doors in the middle, and a distinct vaulting system in each room. In 1612, metropolitan Efrem remade the precinct, adding other wings. The church, presenting the architectural features established in Moldavia since Stephen the Great, plus an open porch, boasts splendid mural paintings, made in 1537. The decorations are late Gothic and Renaissance in style.

Today, the abode is on of UNESCO world heritage list.

Top.
Portal detail with The Mother
of God and the Infant.

Bottom
Window niches with scene
from the Menologion

View from the south: the
open porch of the church
and the monastery museum

67

Sucevita Monastery

The Movila dynasty that would give Moldavia two Princes: Ieremia and Simion, erected the Sucevita Monastery between 1581 and 1601.

The first foundation of this family, which preceded today's monastery complex, was a rather modest church, dating round 1581. Subsequently followed the construction of the abode that we can still admire today.

The monastery consists of a spacious precinct shaped as a quadrilateral, surrounded by tall walls, strengthened by massive corner towers, and also featuring a gate tower. Both the interior and the exterior are decorated by a wealth of remarkable frescoes. Painter Ioan and his brother Sofronie created the paintings before 1596. The monastery is UNESCO world-heritage-listed.

Monastery precinc

pp. 72-
Portal in Gothic style wit
The Holy Trinity, The Ladde
of Divine Virtues (Th
Ladder of St. Joh
Climacus), scenes from th
Genesis, represented in th
upper register on th
northern façac

Monastery church, view from the southwest

The Curtea de Arges Monastery

Neagoe Basarab erected the monastery church between 1514 and 1517 on the place of an older one, while the murals were completed under Radu of Afumati, between 1522 and 1526. The votive plaque, dated September 10, 1526 mentions the name of painter Dobromir. The abode shelters the tombs of the two founding Princes.

The Episcopal Church boasts great architectural value, and a rich ornamentation, with sculpted stone decorations. The two twisted turrets represent a characteristic of the monument.

In the late 19th century, at the initiative of King Carol I, architect Lecomte du Noüy remade the church, with several alterations. The church, a royal necropolis, houses the tombs of Kings Carol I and Ferdinand I, and of Queens Elisabeth and Maria.

Monastery church, view from the southeast

Decorations in sculpted stone

The pronaos of the church

Interior view
Iconostasis

The Three Hierarchs Monastery

Church of the Holy Three Hierarchs Monastery, general view from the south

The Three Hierarchs Church of Iasi (initially a monastery church), a genuine architectural gem, was erected between 1635 and 1639. The founder of this singular monument was Moldavian Prince Vasile Lupu, one of the most consequential figures in the history of the principality, a benefactor and defender of the Eastern Orthodox Church, acknowledged throughout the Balkan Peninsula.

Ornaments sculpted in stone decked the exterior of the church fully, at first the finer work on the façades being covered in gold sheet. Several alterations were brought to the abode in the 19th century, when French architect Lecomte du Noüy restored it.

The funerary slabs of Dimitrie Cantemir, ruler of Moldavia between 1710-1711, and of Alexandru Ioan Cuza, the first sovereign of the United Principalities (1859-1866) can be seen inside the monument.

Lace in sculpted stone. Details

Agapia Monastery

The establishment was founded, between 1642 and 1644 by hetman Gavriil, brother to Prince Vasile Lupu, and is named after the skete of Agapie the Hermit from the 14th century. Architect Enache Ctisi of Constantinople was in charge of the works. Closer to our days, between 1859 and 1862 the proskomediaron, the diaconicon and a new porch were added, the older one being included in the pronaos. There is nothing specific about the architecture of the church, yet the painting of the abode represents a grand asset, being the work of painter Nicolae Grigorescu, between 1858 and 1861. The establishment was restored several times: between 1848 and 1858, when the church underwent several modifications, between 1882 and 1903, when the entire precinct was renewed, and annexed buildings were put up. The monastery boasts a valuable collection of old religious art, and of cult utensils, being an important tourist target in northern Moldavia.

Interior yard, row of cell.

Naos vault, Christ Pantocrator. Church naos St. Ecaterina. Murals by Nicolae Grigorescu

The Wooden Churches of Budesti

The church in the Maramures village of Budesti-Josani was built in oak wood, in 1643, according to the votive inscription at the entrance, and was restored during the 18th century, when it was dedicated to Saint Nicholas. Its architecture is specific for Maramures churches: rectangular plan, polygonal apse, and tall turret with pointed roof above the naos. The outer walls are decorated with frescoes in naïve folk style. The painting dates to 1762.

The church of Budesti-Susani, erected in 1760, and subject to modifications in the 19th century, presents a less interesting architecture. In exchange, the interior painting, achieved by master painter Alexander Ponehalski, in rustic style, is highly valuable.

Overall view fror the southea

Scenes from the Passion of Christ – The Road of the Cross, mural inside the church

Hurezi Monastery

Monastery chapel seen from the west

Erected in the late 17th century by Prince Constantin Brancoveanu, the Hurezi Monastery is one of his most important foundations, and a brilliant example of Brancovan architecture and art. The big church is dedicated to the Hoy Emperors Constantine and Helen. Built between 1691 and 1694, it contains the cenotaph of the Prince, buried in Bucharest secretly, in the St. George Church. The altar screen is in lime wood. The chandelier was ordered in Vienna, and the frescos represent a series of historical characters of the time, from the Brancoveanu, Cantacuzino and Barasab families. The entrance door features a sculpted marble frame. The monastery precinct also includes the Princely house, the library, the cells, etc. Dionisie's belfry, with stolen columns, is an element added later on (1753).

Interior yard, row of cells

Christ Pantocrator, mural on the calotte of the dome

Last Judgment, fresco on the porch of the big church

Details of outer architecture specific for the brancovan style

The Roman-Catholic Cathedral of Alba Iulia

Details from the outer wall

The Roman-Catholic Cathedral of Alba Iulia, dedicated to Saint Archangel Michael, was built in the second half of the 13th century on the spot of an older Romanesque church destroyed by the Tartar invasion of 1241. The abode underwent numerous alterations and restoration jobs along the centuries. St. Archangel Michael, patron of the church is rendered on the main apse, in two bas-reliefs from the 13th century, decorating both walls.

The interior shelters a sarcophagus in carved stone containing the remains of Iancu of Hunedoara, Prince of Transylvania, and a famous anti-Ottoman fighter.

Taken over by the Protestants between 1550 and 1700, the church was later turned Catholic. Important restoration works were carried out in the 20th century. The church organ, dating from 1877, has no less than 2209 tubes.

Interior and exterior view

The Fortified Church of Biertan

The name of the locality was first attested to in 1283, in a document regarding taxes exacted by the Roman-Catholic Chapter of Alba Iulia from the Catholic priests in the Saxon communities.

Erected between 1492 and 1515, the fortified Saxon church of Biertan (dedicated to the Holy Virgin) is a splendid blend of late Gothic and Renaissance elements. Most valuable are the polyptych altar, the sacristy door, and the ornamentation sculpted in stone. The altar features 28 panels with Biblical scenes, in a refined execution, and dates to 1515. That was also the year when the sacristy door was made. The Biertan church is one of the most precious fortified Saxon churches in Romania, included on the heritage list of Transylvanian medieval art and architecture.

Interior view, the polyptych altar and the church vault decorated with terracotta ribbing

Overall view from the east

The Fortified Church of Viscri

Situated in a secluded area, far from the world, the church-citadel of Viscri (in German Weisskirch) was initially a Romanesque basilica, later turned into a hall church. Its construction began in the 13th century, on the spot of a small Romanesque chapel built by Szecklers in 1110.

The church was fortified especially to withhold Turkish attacks. Three towers and two bastions strengthen the interior walls. The two towers, the northern one, on three levels, erected in 1630, and the western one, on four levels, built in 1649, feature defense corridors with a framework parapet covered with planks.

View from the interior yard

Cityscapes

Bucharest – The Romanian Athenaeum

The Romanian Athenaeum opened in 1888. It was erected by public subscription (under the slogan "Give one leu for the Athenaeum!"), on the designs of French architect Albert Galleron, together with Romanian architect C. Baicoianu. The building in neo-classical style has an Ionic fronton and columns. The metal work was the creation of German architect Schwalbach. The big concert hall boasts a circular fresco with scenes from the history of the Romanians, signed by Costin Petrescu.

Inside the building, musical scores of George Enescu's are on display, as well as his violins and pianos, original furniture, library, paintings, engravings, letters, programs, reviews, photos, and documents related to the activity of the great Romanian musician. Between 1919 and 1920 the Athenaeum housed the proceedings of the Chamber of Deputies. Today, it is the headquarters of the George Enescu State Philharmonic.

General view
Bronze statue of poet
Mihai Eminescu, work of
sculptor G. Anghel

Interior view. Athenaeum
Rotunda, a big circular
lobby, doubled by a ring of
12 columns

Details of the exterior architecture: mosaic representations (Prince Neagoe Basarab, King Carol I and Prince Matei Basarab), Ionic fronton and columns

Bucharest – Stavropoleos Church

Situated at the historical core of the capital, right behind the Post Palace (currently the National Museum of History) Stavropoleos Church is a colossal architectural gem. It was built in 1724 by Greek hieromonk Ioanichie, metropolitan of the Stavropola. Subsequent interventions, in various stages, added the porch, the lateral apses and the turret on the naos. The precinct contains a belfry and a several-floor building, erected in the early 20th century on the designs of architect Ion Mincu. The beautiful portico houses tomb slabs and old crosses.

The stone sculptures decorating the exterior, the original iconostasis and frescoes, as well as the exquisite proportions of this perfect example of post-Brancovan art account for the beauty and the harmony of the abode.

The church seen from the inner yard

Inner yard

Details of outer architecture, rich in elements specific for the Brancovan style

Bucharest – The Savings House

Set up as institution during the reign of Prince Cuza, CEC, the Savings House, for a long time a saving and deposit structure, acquired its own headquarters on Victoriei Road, on the place of an older church (St. John the Great) of 1875. Turning too crowded, it was dismantled to make room for the present place, erected between 1896 and 1900, on the designs of French architect Paul Gottereau. The palace still bears the mark of French academism, and has become a genuine symbol of Victoria Road in its glory days. Since 1900, the building has withheld tremors very well, needing no alterations.

Detail of the semicircular fronton

Bucharest - The Cantacuzino Palace

Palace entrance marrying specific elements of French architectural academism, with Rococo and Art Nouveau decorative accents

The Cantacuzino Palace on Victoriei Road (currently the Museum of Music) is also known as the Lion House since two stone lions guard its entrance. Built in the early 20th century according to the designs of architect I. D. Berindei, in French Baroque style, with Rococo elements, above the entrance the edifice features the coat-of-arms of the Cantacuzino family, the Byzantine two-headed eagle.

The palace first belonged to Prince Gheorghe Grigore Cantacuzino, nicknamed the Nabob, former prime minister and mayor of Bucharest, one of the richest persons of his time. The construction was bequeathed to his son, Mihail (Misu), former minister of justice, and his wife, Maruca Cantacuzino, remarried later to great composer George Enescu. In the inter-war period, the Cantacuzino Palace was the headquarters of the Presidency of the Council of Ministers (the government).

Fragment of the palace façade with wrought iron decorations

Interior details with eclectic and Art Nouveau elements

Muse with Harp, detail on the semicircular frontor

Bucharest – The Parliament Palace

Works on the so-called House of the People spanned several years (1984 to 1989), the building stretching on a plot of land obtained by razing an old section of the capital that included monuments of old Romanian architecture. The result was an immense edifice, the first in Europe in point of size (330,000 sq m) and the second in the world, after the Pentagon. Over 80-m high, with twelve floors, at present it houses the two Chambers of Parliament, the International Conference Center, and the National Museum of Contemporary Art.

View from the Heroes' District

p. 113
Façade of the National Museum of Contemporary Art, situated in the wing giving to St. Calea 13 septembrie

Night view

Bucharest – The Cotroceni Palace

In the late 17th century, Prince Serban Cantacuzino erected the Cotroceni Monastery, with a church that survived until the epoch of dictator Ceausescu, who order it demolished. The Princely houses were constructed within the precincts, used now and then by Barbu Stirbey, and, in the 19th century, by Prince Cuza.

King Carol I built the Cotroceni Palace in 1893, and it served as permanent residence for King Ferdinand and Queen Maria. The latter lived here until her death, in 1938. French architect Paul Gottereau created the old wing, while Romanian architect Grigore Cerkez remade the northern wing, after 1900.

Today, one part of the palace has been turned into the Cotroceni National Museum, and the other became, after 1990, the residence of Romania's president. The museum contains valuable collections and some of the palace's old furniture, recovered from the storerooms where they had been deposited after the exile of the royal family.

Exterior view with elements in Byzantine style

Interior view: the refectory

Bucharest – The Village Museum

This museum in the capital city has an extremely picturesque location, on the banks of Herastrau Lake, and is one of the biggest and oldest ethnographic museums throughout Europe. It is the outcome of the endeavors deployed by the Romanian school of sociology, created and brilliantly represented by Dimitrie Gusti, in the interbellum.

The Village Museum was set up in 1936 by bringing 30 peasant homes from their areas of origin, and emplacing them on the border of the Herastru Lake. This perimeter features not only houses but also full households, with annexes, wooden installations, and three windmills. Three old churches can be admired as well. At present, the museum boasts numerous traditional houses, being the biggest open-air museum in Europe.

Genuine rural constructions from all the regions of the country

Building of the Museum of the Romanian Peasant, in neo-Romanian style

In 1912, on the spot of the former State Mint and the Mavrogheni Palace, at the end of Mogosoaia Bridge (Victoriei Plaza) the foundations were laid of the National Art Museum, now the Museum of the Romanian Peasant. Architect N. Ghika-Budesti guided the works.

The building is an excellent illustration of the neo-Romanian style. Its shape reminds of monastic abodes, with arcades, belfry and exposed brick. The central tower, tall and massive, a landmark on Victoriei Road, resembles old monastery belfries. Inside, the spaces are wide, monumental, and the ethnographic collections excellently presented, arranged in an original style by the museum's former director, the regretted painter Horia Bernea. In 1996, the institution received the European Museum of the Year award.

Interior view

Brasov – Council Plaza

The Council House represents the emblematic central building in the Plaza. Mentioned for the first time in 1420, new structures were added to the construction in 1573. The collapse of the tower in 1662 made necessary further works. The big fire of 1689 also caused serious damage.

Throughout the years, the plaza underwent various modifications, especially between 1770 and 1774 when it was defined in Baroque style. The 58-m tall tower, with a guardian role in the history of the town, was erected between 1525 and 1528. At first, the building belonged to the furriers' guild; later it headquartered the Council of the Brasov town. Today, it has been arranged as the county Museum of History.

Council House, Church of the Dormition of the Virgin and the Black Church

The Council House
Facade detail: the town's coat-of-arms

HONTERUS
1498-1549

Brasov – The Black Church

The Black Church of Brasov is the eastern most Gothic cathedral in Europe, and one of the biggest. It was erected between the 14th and the 15th centuries. The construction of the church, in Gothic style, began in 1383, at the time of parish priest Thomas Sander, on the place of an old Romanesque church from the first half of the 13th century. The abode is dedicated to the Holy Virgin but it is known more as the Black Church, in the wake of the 1689 fire that blackened its walls. The tall, narrow windows feature Gothic stone frames, and the exterior buttress are decorated with statues. Inside, a big organ can be seen, as well as a valuable collection of Oriental carpets from the 15th to the 18th centuries. The bronze bell in the belfry weighs six tons.

Panoramic view.
The Black Church in focus

Cluj – The Union Square

The Saint Michael Roman-
Catholic Cathedral.
Overall view

The Saint Michael Roman-Catholic Cathedral (the 14th-15th centuries) has become the trademark of Cluj. This hall-type church received a neo-Gothic tower in 1860. In 1902, a bronze statuary of Matei Corvin, Hungary's King, was placed in front of the cathedral. It is the work of Cluj artist Ianos Fadrusz

The city developed on the place of the ancient settlement of Napoca. As a medieval burg, Cluj (Klausenburg, Kolozsvar) is attested to by documents going back to the 12th-13th centuries. After 1241, Saxons settled here in considerable numbers, so that they exceeded the Hungarians and the Romanians. Later, as a town part of the Austrian Empire, Cluj held the important role of Transylvania's capital. From December 1918, it joined Greater Romania.

Details of the Matei Corvin statuary

Constanta – The Casino

Constanta, rising on the ruins of the ancient Greek colony Tomis, fell, over the centuries, under Byzantine, Genovese, and Ottoman rule. In 1878, it represented the most significant Romanian port at the Black Sea. Its principal assets are the Grand Mosque Carol I, the Hunchiar Mosque, the Museum of History and Archeology, the statue of the Roman poet Ovid, exiled by Emperor Augustus to these parts, and the Roman edifice with mosaic.

Another tourists target in Constanta is the Museum of the Romanian Navy that boasts highly valuable historical and documentary exhibits. Mention could also be made of the Folk Art Museum, and of the Aquarium situated opposite the Casino. This edifice on the seawall was put up in 1909 according to the designs of French architect Daniel Renard, in Art Nouveau style, and represents an emblem of the city.

The Casino.
Details of exterior and interior architecture

The Casino.
General view

Iasi – The Palace of Culture

The city of Iasi is first attested to in a document from the 14th century, when it was just a burg. In the 16th century it became the capital of Moldavia, until the union with Wallachia, in 1859. Iasi was again the capital of the country between 1916 and 1918, when the armies of the Central Powers occupied Bucharest.

In the old center of the city rises the Palace of Culture, a symbol of 20th century Iasi. The construction was carried out between 1905 and 1907, in neo-Gothic style, on the spot of he old princely palace. The building houses a few museums: of history, of ethnography, of nature science, and of technology.

Iasi is rich in memorial houses, included on the list of museums: the house of writer Vasile Pogor, the abode of story teller Ion Creanga, the memorial houses of poet George Toparceanu, of prose writer N. Gane, of poet Mihai Codreanu, of novelist Mihail Sadoveau, of scholar and metropolitan Dosoftei, and others.

Equestrian statue of Stephen the Great; the Palace of Culture in the background

The Palace of Culture

Medias - Evangelical Church

The medieval burg was founded in the 13th century. Strongly fortified by King Matei Corvin, in 1529 the town fell in the hands of Petru Rares for a short time. A few fortifications, parts from the walls and the towers of the stonecutters, blacksmiths, and goldsmiths have been preserved from the old citadel.

An important monument is the fortified Evangelical Church of St. Margareta, erected in the 15th –16th centuries. The church tower (The Trumpeters' Tower) is more than 70 meters high, and comes from the mid 15th century. Inside the church one can admire an old, bronze, christening font, dating to the 14th century. Interesting assets of Media are also the Municipal Museum, with standing exhibitions – of archaeology and history –, and the memorial house of historian S. L. Roth. There are also temporary exhibitions on various topics.

The old center of Medias.
In the background, the St. Margareta Church with the Trumpeter's Towe

The Clock Tower
(The Trumpeters' Tower), detail

Oradea - The historical Centre

Oradea had been an important military and administrative center ever since the 13th-14th centuries. The town boasts numerous architecture monuments; the Roman Catholic Cathedral (the 18th century, the biggest Baroque church in Romania), the Palace with 365 windows (in Baroque style, the 18th century), the Moon Church (an Eastern Orthodox Cathedral from the 18th century), the memorial museums of poet Ady Endre and of journalist Iosif Vulcan, the citadel of Oradea, etc.

The Black Eagle passage dates to 1907-1909 (architect Jakob Dezsö and Komor Marcell). The beautiful Jugendstil stained glass is sure to catch the traveler's eyes.

Under this passage, a troupe of puppeteers delights their young spectators with various stories.

The Town Hall Palace built on the designs of architect Rimanoczy Kalman, in 1902-1903, with strong Jugendstil elements

Buildings in the old center

The Black Eagle Palace; the glass-covered passage, with Jugendstill ornamental elements

Sibiu – The Evangelical Cathedral

The seven-level 70-m tall belfry towers over the Evangelical church

Sibiu (Hermannstadt) is first mentioned in documents from the 12th century as a Saxon town. The fortifications erected in stages surround the upper and the lower towns, around the core represented by the Big Plaza, the Small Plaza, and the Huet Plaza. Besieged twice by the Ottomans in the first half of the 15 century, the burg could resist enemy inroads thanks to its fortifications.

A town of culture, Sibiu benefits from public education institutions (the first school opened here in 1330, then the Jesuit Gymnasium of 1692 – later the Hungarian Gymnasium and today the G. Lazar College), rich collections and libraries. The Brukenthal Museum in Sibiu has excellent collections of classical and folk art, of history, nature science, as well as a valuable library.

Works by artists like Andreas Lapicida, Sebastian Hann, Johann Martin Stock, and Frans Neuhauser can be admired in other parts of the town, too.

Interior of the church. View from the altar

Sibiu – The Big Plaza

The Big Plaza was the heart of the medieval burg, a place for meetings and trade. Public executions were also made here. A remarkable symbol of the town, the Council Tower was erected in 1588 on the place of an older one from the 13th-14th centuries, collapsed by an earthquake. In 1550, a pillory was set up in Big Plaza, a Gothic

monument with Roland's statue at the top, the creation of sculptor Onophorius. Other valuable edifices can also be seen in the Big Plaza: the Holy Trinity Roman-Catholic Church (the 18th century), the Haller House (the 15th-16th centuries), the Reussner House (the 15th-18th centuries), the Bruckenthal Palace (the 18th century).

Sibiu - The Small Plaza

The Small Plaza (also know in the Middle Ages as Circulus parvus) is surrounded by valuable monuments of architecture: the old chemist's shop, The Black Bear, the first of the kind in Romania (today a Museum of the History of Pharmacy, located in a 15th-16th century building), the House of Arts (the former Butcher's Hall, 15th century), the La Turn restaurant (the 15th-16th centuries), the Tower of the Goldsmiths' Stairs (the 15th –16th centuries) under which goes the Goldsmiths' Passage from where steps lead to the Goldsmiths' market, the Hannes House (home to the Franz Binder Museum of World Ethnography, a building dating to 1867). Close by there stands the Emil Sigerus Museum of Saxon Ethnography.

Next to the Big Plaza and the Huet Market, the Small Plaza constitutes the heart of the city, preserving a genuine repository of Transylvanian medieval art.

The Council Tower (1370)

Medieval buildings preserved in original form. On the right stands the beautiful Luxembourg House

Sighisoara - The medieval City

The Clock Tower, view from the
lower town

Sighisoara (Schäessburg) was founded in the 13th century by Saxon colonists. The first citadel, mentioned in 1280, was erected on an elevated plateau, serving as refuge for the inhabitants of this settlement at the foot of the hill. It was endowed with fortifications, of which parts of walls and defense towers have been preserved.

The Tower Clock, the darling of the town, dates back to the 14th century. About 64-m tall, it is built in Baroque style, characteristic after the big fire of 1676.

One of the few civil constructions preserved from before the big fire is the House of Vlad Dracul where the Wallachian Prince, father to Vlad Tepes, known in the West as Dracula, supposedly lived for a while.

The Clock Tower, details

Targu Jiu – The Monumental Ensemble

The town is important for the original collection of sculptures signed by Constantin Brancusi (1876-1957), the most well-known Romanian sculptor, born in the village of Hobita, close to Targu Jiu. He created several statuaries here, towards the end of the 1930s, in memory of the Romanian soldiers fallen in the First World War: The Table of Silence, The Alley of Chairs, The Gate of the Kiss, The Endless Column, and The Festive Table (a smaller variant of The Table of Silence).

The monuments have been deployed on an axis, in a succession that is not accidental but reveals essential moments of life.

The Endless Column reminds of the massive woodcarvings, with rhombic motifs, on the porches of Gorj peasant houses.

The Brancusi sculptural ensemble: The Table of Silence made of limestone, with twelve chairs, The Endless Column, a true axis mundi, and The Gate of the Kiss, sculpted in Banpotoc travertine

Targu Mures
The Prefect's Palace and the Palace of Culture

The Prefect's Palace,
general view

The monumental building of the Prefect's Office was erected between 1905 and 1907, to house the town hall. Bearing the imprint of Jugendstil, the palace tower, 60 meters tall, was at first the fire belfry of Targu Mures.

The Palace of Culture was put up between 1911 and 1913, and stands out by its special decorations: frescoes, bas-reliefs, the blue-white-pink majolica roof, the monumental mosaic.

The lobby is decorated with Venetian mirrors. The Hall of Mirrors features six highly valuable stained glass panes. The three-floor construction has a remarkable façade owing in particular to the mosaic made after the drawings of painter Aladár Körösföi Kreisch. The Palace of Culture houses today the Art Museum of the town.

The Palace of Culture, exterior
details with specific Jugendstil
architectural elements

Timisoara - The historical Centre

Timisoara was first attested to by a document from 1212. After the conquest of Belgrade, in 1521, Italian architects rapidly fortified Timisoara. At least three gate towers are known to have been transformed at that time.

In 1716, the armies of Prince Eugene of Savoy conquered Timisoara. The Turks were driven away, and the town joined the Hapsburg Empire for two centuries, being massively colonized with Catholic Germans (Swabians). The representative buildings of Timisoara, giving the city a Baroque air, came from the early 18th century, too.

King Mihai I, in the presence of the time's premier solemnly inaugurated the Eastern Orthodox Cathedral, in 1946.

The Union Square, the Roman-Catholic Cathedral and the Holy Trinity Statue

The Union Square and the statue of the Holy Trinity

Victoriei Plaza, exterior details of the buildings
Dauerbach Palace, façade to the park

The metropolitan cathedral dedicated to the Three Hierarchs

Nature's Spectacle

Bukovina

The churches and monasteries of Bukovina date from the time of the first Musat rulers, and came to great artistic splendor during the reign of Stephen the Great and Petru Rares. Numerous exterior frescoes to be found on the most famous churches and monasteries in the region go back to the time of Petru Rares.

A wooded realm, Bukovina has diversified relief contours, with soft heights and sheltered valleys mostly, where settlements are situated. Traditional crafts like pottery and woodcarving have come down to our time. Another famous artistic trade is that of decorating Easter eggs, famous not only throughout the country but also abroad.

The natural splendors of the region and its numerous tourist targets of universal value turn Bukovina into a prime-time tourist destination.

Landscape in the area of Sucevita Monastery

Traditional houses in Bukovina

The Rucar-Bran Corridor

This corridor crosses the Southern Carpathians, connecting Wallachia to Transylvania. It stretches between the localities of Bran – with its celebrated castle – and Rucar, an area known for its perfectly preserved folk traditions. Folk costumes have remained unchanged for centuries, and customs are vivid and genuine. Nature is generous and the sceneries magnificent.

Agrotourism has developed considerably in the area, in such localities as Fundata, Sirnea or Moeciu. They provide all-year accommodation in nice boarding houses, from where tourists have numerous possibilities to start trekking or otherwise relax. The main trade in the region is sheep tending, for which reason the delicious cheese produced here is yet another fine advertisement.

Views from the Rucar-Bran corridor

Fundata, Bucegi Mountains

The Piatra Craiului Mountains

The National Piatra Craiului Park situated in the Southern Carpathians, in the Arges and Brasov Counties, includes the Piatra Craiului Massif and the Dambovicioara and Dambovita gorges. Amazingly picturesque, the park boasts numerous special flora and fauna species.

The Piatra Craiului Massif stands in contrast to the surrounding mountains (Fagaras, Iezer, Bucegi) owing to its daring silhouette, its position across the Southern Carpathians, and its maximum height of 2238 meters. The Piatra Craiului Mountains feature the tallest calcareous crest in Romania that gives the range a spectacular air. The steep slopes represent a favorite target with mountaineers, and escalades are fully awarded by the formidable view the summit affords.

Winter in the Piatra Craiului Mountains reserve

The Miracle from the Depths

Emil Racovita, a polymath, laid the foundations of a new discipline, biospeleology, in 1907, and in 1920 he founded in Cluj, the first Speleology Institute in the world. Animated by the inquisitive spirit of their mentor, Racovita's followers have begun extensive exploration of the karstic regions in Romania. Thanks to them the number of caves studied has risen from nearly 500 in Racovita's time, to over 12,000 nowadays, which places Romania in the top echelon in Europe. Many of these caves are tens of kilometers long, and a few hundreds meters deep. They hide gigantic halls, rivers and lakes, rare minerals, fossils of long-gone species, numerous traces of the early days of humankind, from the Paleolithic to the Middle Ages, all in all, a formidable geographic dimension continually expanding, with a huge scientific, tourist, and exploratory potential.

Rece Cave, Apuseni Mountains, 2.5-m high very frail fistuliform stalactites

pp.166-167
Cadanelor Basins, the Topolnita-Epuran system, Mehedinti Plateau. Waters have submerged a forest of stalagmites forming an underground mineral delta

Church Hall, the Scarisoara Glacier. Ice madonnas, saints, and altars grow under the arched vault of the hall

The Trans-Fagaras Road

This road laid between 1970 and 1974 crosses the Fagaras Mountains in the Southern Carpathians, going south from Transylvania (Cartisoara locality), to Wallachia, to Curtea de Arges. Between October and June, the road, with numerous tunnels and viaducts, is closed because of the snow.

First, the highway goes along the Cartisoara River, passes by the Balea Waterfall (40-m high) and reaches Balea Lake, the highest glacier lake in Fagaras Mountains. The area features other glacier lakes as well: Capra, Caprita, and Caltun. On the southern slope of the Fagaras, the Capra Waterfall, together with the Vidraru Lake and Dam, represent other spectacular objectives.

Vidaru Lake provides recreation facilities and comfortable accommodation in the chalets on its banks (Casa Argeseana, Valea cu Pesti, Cumpana, and others).

View of the section between Balea Lake and Waterfall, from the northern side of the Fagaras Mountains

Capra Waterfall on the southern side of the Fagaras Mountains

The Danube Gorges

The Danube Gorges, Dacian Prince Decebalus sculpted in the mountain, and ruins of the Tri-Kule citadel

Called Cazane (Cauldrons in Romanian), these gorges stretching on 45 kilometers, make up a well individualized geomorphic unit, divided into two distinct parts: the Big and the Small Cazane, with a breathtaking natural view.

The Big Cazane extend on 3.8 kilometers, and are created by the Ciucaru Mare Hill the steep slopes of which border the left side of the river, and by Stirbatul Mare Hill, situating in Serbia. From the Ciucarului Mare plateau an ample and amazing panorama opens up over the big gorges. Between the Dubova basinet and Ogradena there rise the Small Cazane.

The flora of the area includes many sub-Mediterranean elements mingled to central European ones, as well as protected species, such as the European yew (Taxus baccata), a monument of nature. Karstic relief is well represented by surface and depth formations (several caves have been identified, of which the most important is Ponicova).

The Apuseni Mountains

The Apuseni Mountains, in the Western Carpathians, situated between the valleys of the Somes and Mures rivers, do not stand taller than 1849 m (Cucurbata Mare Peak). Made up of limestone, the Apuseni, thanks to their geological structure provide a wide variety of original natural formations and sceneries: caves (Scarisoara, the Bears' Cave), underground springs, and spectacular gorges. The mild height and slopes are a characteristic of Apuseni landscape.

The region, mainly rural, with rare settlements, is inhabited by Motzi, highlanders with ancestral habits, and traditional occupations like sheep breeding, wood processing and mining. Some of the mines here, famous for their gold and non-ferrous metals ever since the time of the Romans, are still continuing the tradition.

Landscapes in the
Apuseni Mountains

Maramures

Maramures has variegated relief contours, with the heights of Gutai, Tibles, Maramures, and Rodna mountains prevailing. The valleys of Isa, Viseu, and Mara cross the Maramures depression. Along these valleys, an old civilization developed organically and flourished, with a material creation that is profoundly religious. Using in principal wood to build tall and svelte churches, covered with shingles and painted on the inside, the people of Maramures have preserved unaltered their Eastern Orthodox faith, their ancient customs and costumes that they still wear on festivals.

Maramures can take pride in rich mineral resources (gold, silver, copper, lead). Historically, ethnographically, and touristically, the region is divided into four areas; the Land of Maramures, the Land of Lapus, the Land of Chioar, and Baia Mare.

Village Museum in Sighetul Marmatiei, peasant architecture specific to the region

The Danube Delta

A unique natural reserve in Europe and a major tourist attraction, the Danube Delta represents a true paradise of the flora and fauna, with sights unaltered by man's intervention. Stretching between the arms of the Danube, Chilia, Sulina, and St. George, on nearly 5000 sq km, the Delta is a young land geologically speaking, formed from the deposits brought by the river when flowing into the Black Sea.

The Danube Delta represents the natural environment of a host of vegetal species (the most common are reef, white willow, and sedge) and animals. In spring and in autumn, no less than 300 species of birds, many migratory, can be seen nesting here. Then the Delta is also a haven for fishermen, given the considerable number of fish found here.

In 1990, UNESCO included the Danube Delta, the newest formed relief contour in Romania, among the biosphere reserves, safe from industrialization.

Fishing on the
Danube canals

Pelican's colony

The Black Sea Shore

The Romanian coast of the Black Sea covers 245 kilometers and stretches between the arms of Chilia to the north, and the border with Bulgaria to the south. The area with biggest tourist potential lies between Cape Midia to the north and Vama Veche to the south, most of the resorts being situated south of Constanta. Some of them date to the early 20th century (Mamaia, Eforie Sud/Carmen Sylva); others were built after WW2 (Olimp, Saturn, Venus, Neptun). The resorts on the seashore benefit from natural elements like mud and aerosols.

The most important towns on the Romanian seacoast are Constanta and Mangalia, with interesting historical monuments (Greek-Roman, Byzantine, Genovese, and Ottoman) and modern accommodation potential. At the same time, they are the most important Romanian maritime ports.

Mamaia resort

The beach and hotels
in Olimp resort

Text
Daniel Focşa
Dana Voiculescu

Photograph Credits
Dan Ioan Dinescu
Mircea Savu
Ovidiu Morar

Bird's eye Photographs
Ştefan Petrescu

English version
Alina Cârâc

Editing and captions
Irina Spirescu

Graphic design
Adrian Sorin Georgescu

DTP
Enciu Roxana

Project co-ordinator
Ovidiu Morar
Arpad Harangozo

Our thanks to Mr Cristian Lascu for his support in the achievement
of the "The Miracle from the Depths" section

Printed by R.A. Monitorul Oficial

© NOI Media Print
Str. Tokyo, Nr 1
Sector 1, Bucureşti
Tel.: 021 222 07 34
Fax: 021 222 07 86
e-mail: nmp@nmp.ro
www.nmp.ro